To:

_____

From:

_____

Date:

_____

a collection of stories,
quotes, scriptures,
and inspirational
thoughts

a

Touch

of love to celebrate friendship

HOWARD
PUBLISHING CO.

A Touch of Love to Celebrate Friendship © 2002 by Howard Publishing Company
All rights reserved. Printed in the United States of America

Published by Howard Publishing Co., Inc.,
3117 North 7th Street, West Monroe, LA 71291-2227

02 03 04 05 06 07 08 09 10 11   10 9 8 7 6 5 4 3 2 1

Concept by Clay Young and Paul Shepherd
Stories and messages by Ginger Young
Edited by Michele Buckingham

ISBN: 1-58229-263-9

Unless otherwise noted, Scripture quotations are taken from the Holy Bible, New International Version, copy-
right © 1973, 1978, 1984 International Bible Society. Used by permission of Zondervan Bible Publishers.
Scriptures marked ASV are taken from the American Standard Version of the Holy Bible.

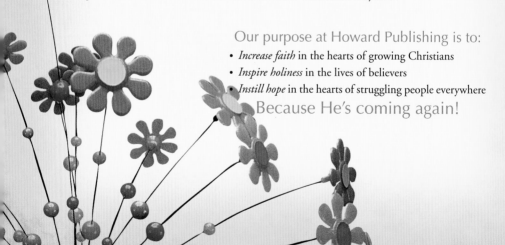

Our purpose at Howard Publishing is to:
- *Increase faith* in the hearts of growing Christians
- *Inspire holiness* in the lives of believers
- *Instill hope* in the hearts of struggling people everywhere

Because He's coming again!

A Touch of Love to

Celebrate Friendship

v

Forever
Real
Inspiring
Encouraging
Never Failing
Delightful
Supportive

CHAPTER 1

Forever

Standing and gazing into the starry night sky, we can see that the darkness of space goes on forever—from here to a never, never finish. The expanse of space has no boundary; there is nothing to define its end. Forever friendship carries this same impression of vast expanse. Where the friendship began doesn't matter, for now no ending is in sight. There is no limit to its duration.

From the beginning of time, people have found friendship to be a source of strength for facing the joys and struggles of life. True friends grow together as they grow gracefully old together, helping one another live life to the fullest.

That's what you are—my friend forever.

Who by his understanding made the heavens,

His love endures forever.

who spread out the earth upon the waters,

His love endures forever.

who made the great lights—

His love endures forever.

the sun to govern the day,

His love endures forever.

the moon and stars to govern the night;

His love endures forever.

—Psalm 136:5–9

Yes, we must ever be friends;
and of all who offer you friendship
let me be ever the first,
the truest, the nearest and dearest!

—Henry Wadsworth Longfellow

A Forever Kind of Love

Fourteen-year-old Cassandra sat on the front porch step, her elbows on her knees, her head resting in her hands. Her unhappiness was evident in the loud sigh that escaped from her lips without restraint. She kicked a rock with her foot, allowing the random act to be an outlet for her frustration.

Why did my parents allow me to be placed in this foster home? she silently fumed. *How could they abandon me? Why couldn't they control their anger? Why did that nosy neighbor have to call the police the night my dad hit my mom? Why can't anyone in my life really love me—with a forever kind of love?*

Meanwhile, in the house across the street, Ann Quincy was clearing the lunch dishes from her kitchen table. Her daughter and two grandchildren had come for a visit earlier in the day, and she had stayed so busy playing with the children that she had postponed the cleanup. Now, as she washed the last few cups and plates, she gazed

Chapter One: *Forever*

out the window that was just above her sink. *Who is that thin, sad-looking teenager sitting on the steps of the Oakley house?* she wondered. To Ann, a widow for twelve years, the girl appeared lonely, as if she didn't have a friend in the world.

She must be the Oakleys' new foster child, Ann concluded, putting down her dishrag. Then, filling a plate with some of the cookies left over from lunch, she quickly headed across the street to meet her new neighbor.

The sound of a door slamming shut startled Cassandra out of her dark thoughts for a moment. Looking up, she studied the woman who was now crossing the street and coming her way. *Just some old lady. Nobody I need to know,* she decided, wrapping herself again in the blanket of self-pity that had become so familiar.

As the woman came up the walk toward Cassandra, she spoke cheerily. "Hi. I'm Ann Quincy. Welcome to the neighborhood! I brought you some chocolate chip cookies. I baked them just this morning."

By the time Cassandra realized that the woman was speaking to her, Ann had seated herself on the step right beside her. Cassandra looked up to see a kind, smiling face looking her squarely in the eyes. She was so surprised that she had to stop and think how to respond.

"I…I'm Cassandra Fletcher," she stammered. "Uh, thank you for the cookies."

"You're welcome. When you finish them, bring the plate back and stay for a visit," Ann instructed, with a warmth and sincerity that made Cassandra suspect the woman really meant it. "And tell Mike and Sarah I'll send more over for them when you return the plate."

Cassandra picked up a cookie and began nibbling on the edges as she watched her new acquaintance walk back across the street. *If she thinks she can get me to like her, she can forget it! Everyone I've ever liked has let me down,* she thought. *Maybe Ann Quincy is just an old, nosy neighbor like the one who called the police on my parents.*

The next day after school, Sarah Oakley, Cassandra's foster mother, gave Cassandra the assignment of returning the empty plate.

"Mike loves Miss Ann's cookies, so if you'll run across the street and bring back those cookies she promised, we'll have them for dessert tonight with ice cream. Thanks," Sarah said, smiling and walking out of the room before Cassandra could protest. Sarah knew that Ann would find a way to get this quiet, unhappy girl to stay and talk for at least a few minutes.

Reluctantly Cassandra headed toward the Quincy house, plate in hand. She stepped onto the porch, hesitated a moment, then knocked

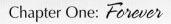

gently on the door. *If I'm lucky, no one will answer,* she thought. *One thing's for sure: I'm not going to hang around and visit with this old lady. I don't care if it means dessert or not.*

The door swung open, and before Cassandra knew it, Ann Quincy was standing next to her on the porch. "Oh, I am so glad you came for a visit! Put the plate on the table next to the door and follow me," she said, scurrying down the porch steps and around the corner of the house into the backyard.

Cassandra had no choice but to follow. Hurrying to keep up, she rounded the corner and then stopped with a

gasp. There before her eyes was the most beautiful flower garden she had ever seen. In the middle of the garden was a small pond with a waterfall flowing gently over a wall of smooth gray stones.

"Do you have any fish in the pond?" Cassandra heard herself ask as she stepped to the edge of the pond and peered into the water. *I'll just stay for a minute and no longer,* she promised herself.

"Oh, yes, and they're starving," Mrs. Quincy said as she stooped down to tug at a weed. "The food is there in the green bucket. Why don't you give them a scoop?"

"Oh, I couldn't. I don't know how. I've never done anything like that," Cassandra protested. Then she lowered her head and added, "I'm not very good at taking care of things."

"There's no way to do it wrong," Ann insisted cheerily, turning her back to Cassandra so the girl could feed the fish without feeling watched.

Cautiously, Cassandra picked up the scoop and shook the small brown pellets across the water. When the fish rushed to the surface to eat their meal, Cassandra's eyes widened. She knelt beside the pond and watched with awe.

After a few moments, Ann called out, "Pick up a spade, why don't you, and help me weed. I need to finish before dark."

Chapter One: *Forever*

Cassandra turned and looked at the old woman who was now bent over in the garden, her face and hands already smeared with dirt. Not knowing what else to do, Cassandra picked up a spade from a nearby tool basket.

"I don't know how to do this," Cassandra said.

"I'll show you," Ann responded.

By the time the sun was setting, the quiet teenager had weeded a large patch of the flower bed. She had also confided to Ann that she was struggling in math at school.

Ann stood up slowly, put her hands on her hips, and surveyed the garden. "Isn't it beautiful now?" she said. "You did a wonderful job. Thanks! I couldn't have finished without you." Then she promised to help Cassandra with her math lesson after dinner the next day.

Over the weeks that followed, Cassandra's visits to the garden became a habit, and little by little she began to open up to Ann about the problems in her family. Ann just listened, commenting only to praise Cassandra for the job she'd done on her assigned chore that day. Ann ended every visit with the same words: "Thanks! I couldn't have finished without you."

During the three years that Cassandra remained with the Oakleys, the friendship between the two gardeners was nurtured even more carefully than the garden they tended. Before long, Cassandra didn't need an invitation to visit Ann or to work in the garden. She knew she was as welcome in the Quincy home as she was at the Oakleys'. She was beginning to believe that she might be loveable after all—that maybe someone really could love her with a forever kind of love.

As her senior year came to an end, Cassandra worked side by side with Ann to make sure the garden looked its best for the party they'd planned for the morning of graduation. The Oakleys and the Quincys—Ann's daughter and grandchildren—were going to have brunch next to the pond and then attend the graduation ceremony together.

The afternoon before graduation, the two spent extra time in the garden. They wanted everything to be perfect for Cassandra's special day. Finally, as the sun disappeared below the horizon, Ann stood up and said, "There! We're done. Thanks for all your help, Cassie. You did a great job around the edges of the pond. I couldn't have finished without you."

Then Ann disappeared around the corner of the house and returned with a beautiful flowering plant in a ceramic pot.

"Here, Cassandra. I potted this for you," she said. "It's one of the ones we planted three years ago when you first moved into our neighborhood. Keep it in your dorm room next year as a reminder of our garden and how much you've grown."

Cassandra took the pot in her arms, looked deeply into the eyes of the old woman she had come to love so much, and knew that she was now equipped to love others with an unconditional, forever kind of love—the kind of love that Miss Ann had extended to her.

It was dark now, and the streetlights had come on. Cassandra started for home but stopped abruptly when she reached the middle of the street. Turning, she saw Ann still standing on the porch, watching her.

"Don't forget your camera in the morning, Miss Ann," she called out. "And about my graduation—thanks. I couldn't have finished without you."

Then, smiling, she bounced up the steps to the Oakleys' front door, knowing Ann wouldn't have time to reply.

Celebrate the happiness

that friends are always giving,

Make every day a holiday and celebrate just living!

—Amanda Bradley

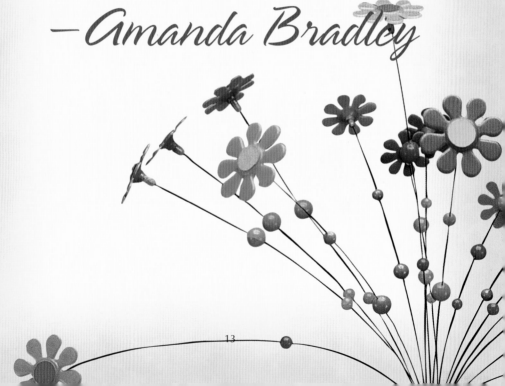

13

The mere process of growing old together
will make the slightest acquaintance
seem a bosom friend.

— Logan Pearsall Smith

The LORD will watch over your coming and going both now and forevermore.

—Psalm 121:8

JOHN 15:13

Greater love has no one than this,

that he lay down his life for his

friends.

Forever
Real
Inspiring
Encouraging
Never Failing
Delightful
Supportive

CHAPTER 2

Real

What does it mean to be "real"? The dictionary defines *real* as "authentic, genuine." *Real* is the spirit of true friendship. Real friends stick with you through thick and thin. They see a need and meet it. They wash your dishes when you're in a rush and take out your trash when you're sick. They're there for you when your nail is broken *and* when your heart is broken. Real friends don't just say they care; they show they care.

I'm thankful our friendship is authentic and genuine. Thanks for being a real friend.

PROVERBS 17:17

A friend
loves at all times.

Everyone hears what you say.

Friends listen to what you say.

Best friends listen to what you don't say.

—Anonymous

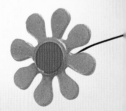

A REAL FRIEND

*A simple friend doesn't know your parents' first names.
A real friend has their phone numbers
in his address book.*

*A simple friend brings a hostess gift to your party.
A real friend comes early to help you cook
and stays late to help you clean.*

*A simple friend hates it when you call after
he has gone to bed.
A real friend asks you why you took so long to call.*

A simple friend seeks to talk with you
about your problems.
A real friend seeks to help you with your problems.

A simple friend wonders about your romantic history.
A real friend could blackmail you with it.

A simple friend, when visiting, acts like a guest.
A real friend opens your refrigerator and helps himself.

A simple friend thinks the friendship is
over when you have an argument.
A real friend knows that it's not a friendship
until after you've had a fight.

A simple friend expects you to always be there for him.
A real friend expects to always be there for you!

—Anonymous

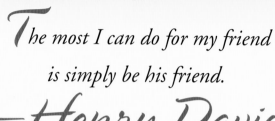

The most I can do for my friend

is simply be his friend.

—Henry David Thoreau

A despairing man should have

the devotion of

his friends.

—Job 6:14

Forever
Real
Inspiring
Encouraging
Never Failing
Delightful
Supportive

CHAPTER 3

Inspiring

Niagara Falls is a place of amazing beauty, power, and inspiration. The Appalachian Mountains are inspirational, too. So is the Painted Desert. And who can look out over the Grand Canyon without feeling inspired?

All of these natural wonders have the ability to inspire us with a sense of awe, courage, and hope. Friendship is meant to inspire in the same way. True friends inspire us to be courageous and hopeful through both the successes and tragedies of life. They inspire us to persevere and rejoice in the big events as well as in the mundane tasks of every day.

I can say without reservation: You are an inspiration! When I grow up, I want to be just like you.

A friend may well be reckoned the masterpiece of nature.

—Ralph Waldo Emerson

Holy, holy, holy

is the LORD Almighty;

The whole earth is full

of his glory.

—Isaiah 6:3

*If we all did the things
we are capable of doing,
we would literally astound ourselves.*

—Thomas Edison

Friendship needs no studied phrases,
Polished face, or winning wiles;
Friendship deals no lavish praises,
Friendship dons no surface smiles.

Friendship follows nature's diction,
Shuns the blandishments of art,
Boldly severs truth from fiction,
Speaks the language of the heart.

Friendship favors no condition,
Scorns a narrow-minded creed,
Lovingly fulfills its mission,
Be it word or be it deed.

Friendship cheers the faint and weary,
Makes the timid spirit brave,
Warns the erring, lights the dreary,
Smooths the passage to the grave.

Friendship—pure, unselfish friendship,
All through life's allotted span,
Nurtures, strengthens, widens, lengthens,
Man's relationship with man.

—Unknown

PROVERBS 27:17

As iron sharpens iron,

so one man

sharpens another.

Character is not made on the mountaintops of life; it is made in the valleys.

—Kathryn Kuhlman

38

The friendship
of Jehovah is with them
that fear him.

—Psalm 25:14 ASV

Forever

Real

Inspiring

Encouraging

Never Failing

Delightful

Supportive

CHAPTER 4

Encouraging

"Go for it! You can do it!"

We all need a cheerleader! On a sports team, the person who provides encouragement is as crucial as any player. To keep the goal in sight and remind the players to keep pushing toward it: That's a role that takes as much energy and vitality as any on the field.

In the game of life, friends are the ones who give us the little pushes of encouragement we need from time to time. True friends stand by us in the fourth quarter—even when the other side has the advantage—and cheer, "Keep moving! You'll be a better person for having finished the game!"

You, my friend, are a great encourager.

HEBREWS 3:13

Encourage one another

daily, as long as

it is called Today.

*R*eal friendship is shown
in times of trouble;
prosperity is full of friends.

—*Euripides*

Courage Made New

Encouragement doesn't always walk in the front door, Michelle thought to herself as she waited on the sidewalk outside Shelby's school. The bell rang, and she smiled as she watched Shelby bound out of the school building and run down the steps in excitement.

"Can we get an ice cream cone before we go to the zoo?" Shelby asked as she took Michelle's hand.

"Sure. What flavor do you want?" Michelle said, knowing the answer before she asked the question.

"Strawberry," Shelby said, smiling. "Pink is my favorite color."

As they walked to the car, Michelle thought back to the first time she met her special friend. It had been Michelle's first Sunday teaching the third-grade class at church. The preceding months had been the most difficult of her whole life. Her husband of fourteen years had left her for a woman half his age. Michelle felt like a discarded, out-of-style, old dress. She had neither hope nor courage until her counselor had told her that giving of herself to others might help her overcome the depression that had overtaken her life. That's how she had found herself in a classroom full of eight-year-olds.

When Shelby's mother had entered the room, she escorted her daughter to a seat on the back row. Michelle hadn't been able to keep herself from staring at her new student. A creeping dread filled her mind as she imagined the demands that

would be placed on her in the months to come. *She's not going to be able to learn what I have to teach.*

Seeing the expression on her teacher's face, Shelby had looked directly into Michelle's eyes and said, "I'm taller than everybody else, so I have to sit in the back."

The other children hadn't seemed to think anything was out of the ordinary. They accepted this special classmate as they would any other. Disappointed in herself for her initial reaction, Michelle had silently promised to make up for any harm she may have done.

Shelby was special. She had been born with Down syndrome. She was twenty-one years old, and Michelle soon found that Shelby was in precisely the right class for her ability.

From that day on, Michelle kept her promise. She made sure that she spoke to Shelby every time she saw her. She took the time to find out Shelby's favorite Bible story books and read aloud from them in class. She baked cookies and let Shelby hand them out to the other students. Once Shelby's mother knew that Shelby was comfortable being alone with Michelle, she allowed Michelle to take her daughter on special outings—like the one to the zoo today. Now Michelle

Chapter Four: *Encouraging*

made it a point to do something special with Shelby at least once a week so her mother could have time for herself.

Michelle's counselor had been right. As she gave of her heart and time to Shelby, her own heart was encouraged and brightened, and her depression began to slowly fade.

Shelby called Michelle her best friend and drew pictures and made cards for her frequently. Michelle's favorite was the one that read, "I never had a friend before you." Michelle framed the card and hung it in a special spot on her kitchen wall.

Shelby had a joyous and thankful attitude about everything she did. She loved the wind blowing across her face. She liked to stop and listen to the rustling of the leaves as she and Michelle walked in the park. She always spoke to the elderly people sitting on the benches and asked how they were feeling.

Thanks to Shelby, Michelle was once again seeing the beauty of God's creation. She was even finding new joy in the activities she had loved as a child. Today's trip to see the lions, tigers, and bears was as exciting for her as it was for Shelby!

When their tour of the zoo was almost completed, Shelby stopped, took Michelle's hand, and asked, "Michelle, why do you want to be my friend?"

"You make me happy when we're together, Shelby," Michelle replied, curious about the question. "Why do you ask?"

"I'm different from your other friends. Do you play with me just because you feel sorry for me?"

Shelby looked deep into Michelle's eyes for an answer. And for a moment Michelle felt shame, remembering the way she had reacted when the two first met.

"Well, maybe I did the day I first met you, when you walked into my Sunday school class," Michelle said honestly. "Now I know that the only people I feel sorry for are the people who don't know how special you are."

"Shelby," Michelle continued, "I don't know if this will make sense to you, but your friendship made me very happy at a time when I felt sad and lonely. You *encourage* me."

"What's that mean?" Shelby inquired, crinkling up her nose quizzically.

"*Encourage* means to make someone feel brave and strong when they were feeling weak and afraid. Do you understand?"

Shelby smiled broadly and her eyes filled with a wisdom beyond her mental years. "I understand, Miss Michelle, 'cause you *courage* me too!"

*A real friend is one who walks in
when the rest of
the world walks out.*

— *Anonymous*

Therefore encourage one another

and build each other up,

just as in fact you are doing.

—1 Thessalonians 5:11

Forever
Real
Inspiring
Encouraging
Never Failing
Delightful
Supportive

CHAPTER 5

Never Failing

It's always a blessing to find a friend. It's a greater blessing when two people grow together and become *never-failing* friends—the kind that stick together through thick and thin.

Never-failing friends are available whenever you need them. They understand you and accept you the way you are. They're your champions when you're in the right, and they care enough to tell you when you're in the wrong. But right or wrong, they stay in your corner. Never-failing friends never fail to love.

You have been—and still are—my never-failing friend.

L A M E N T A T I O N S   3 : 2 2 – 2 3

Because of the LORD's great love

we are not consumed,

for his compassions never fail.

They are new every morning;

great is your faithfulness.

The world is blessed by people who do things, and not by those who merely talk about them.

—James Oliver

He who loves
a pure heart and
whose speech is gracious
will have the king
for his friend.

—Proverbs 22:11

Friends are God's way
of taking care of us.

—Anonymous

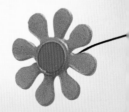

When trouble comes your soul to try,
You love the friend who just "stands by."
Perhaps there's nothing he can do—
The thing is strictly up to you;

For there are troubles all your own,
And paths the soul must tread alone;
Times when love cannot smooth the road
Nor friendship lift the heavy load,

But just to know you have a friend
Who will "stand by" until the end,
Whose sympathy through all endures,
Whose warm handclasp is always yours—

It helps, someway, to pull you through,
Although there's nothing he can do.
And so with fervent heart you cry,
"God bless the friend who just 'stands by'!"

—B. Y. Williams

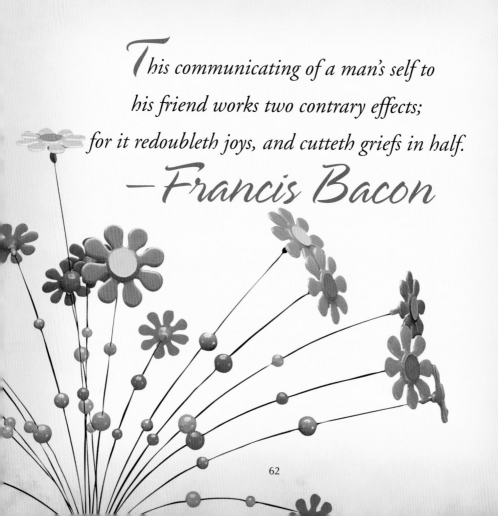

This communicating of a man's self to his friend works two contrary effects; for it redoubleth joys, and cutteth griefs in half.

— *Francis Bacon*

As surely as the LORD lives

and as you live,

I will not leave you.

—2 Kings 2:2

Two are better than one,

because they have a good return for their work:

If one falls down, his friend can help him up.

But pity the man who falls

and has no one to help him up!

Also, if two lie down together,

they will keep warm.

But how can one keep warm alone?

Though one may be overpowered,

two can defend themselves.

A cord of three strands is not quickly broken.

—Ecclesiastes 4:9–12

Forever
Real
Inspiring
Encouraging
Never Failing
Delightful
Supportive

CHAPTER 6

Delightful

Some of our best days are the ones we spend relaxing and having fun with friends. Those special times of perfect peace and sheer enjoyment help to refresh our spirits and make everyday pressures abate for a while. Such moments are as necessary to our survival as eating. They are simply delightful—and so are the friends we share them with.

Pure delight—that's you!

PHILIPPIANS 1:3

I thank my God

every time

I remember you.

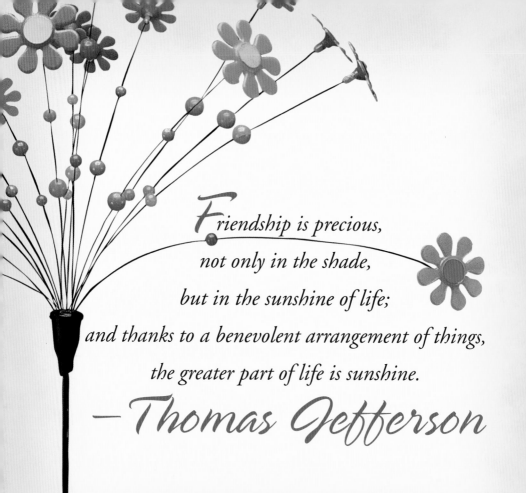

Friendship is precious,

not only in the shade,

but in the sunshine of life;

and thanks to a benevolent arrangement of things,

the greater part of life is sunshine.

— Thomas Jefferson

70

A Day of Beauty

Paige and Madeline had been looking forward to this day for three weeks. This was going to be *their* day—a day of total indulgence. They got the idea from another close friend, Faye, who had received a coupon for "a day of beauty" at a local spa as a birthday gift.

"I felt like a new woman after all that primping and preening," Faye had enthused. "The mud bath was wonderful. I can't even begin to tell you what it did for my legs! And I could see an immediate difference after the facial. See, my skin tone is so much rosier." She had pulled back her hair so that Paige and Madeline could agree with her assessment. "I loved having my nails done," she continued. "It made me feel so elegant. You two just have to try it!"

Neither Paige nor Madeline had ever had a professional manicure or pedicure, much less a facial. The closest Paige had come to having a mud bath was during the previous summer when her children dug a hole in the backyard; she nearly fell into it one afternoon after a hard rain.

Chapter Six: *Delightful*

As Faye continued to describe her day of luxurious treatment at the spa, the two friends grew more and more certain that they wanted to plan an entire day of pampering, too. After all, didn't they need an immediate improvement in skin tone just as much as Faye did?

They agreed upon a date, made their plans, and then waited for the day with great anticipation. Somehow just seeing "Day of Beauty" written on their calendars in black and white made the routines and responsibilities of their daily lives seem lighter.

A Day of Beauty

Finally their special day arrived. The pampering began with a manicure, followed by a brunch of fresh fruit, quiche, and sparkling water—a far cry from their usual lunch of yogurt or peanut butter and jelly—and a luscious dessert called "Chocolate Bombe." Next came the facial masque; and while Paige and Madeline reclined in comfortable lounge chairs, thin slices of cucumber covering their eyes, their feet soaked in a special bath of perfumed salts that released the scent of freesia into the air. The two women sighed. The day was turning out to be every bit as wonderful as they had expected.

"What has been your favorite part of the day?" Madeline asked, moving her lips ever so slightly to keep from disturbing the masque and cucumbers.

Paige thought for a moment. "I think what we're doing now—lying here with our feet soaking, smelling these wonderful smells, feeling so relaxed. And this facial feels so good. I wonder if I'll still see the bags under my eyes from staying up with the baby last night. Aren't these cucumber slices supposed to take care of that?"

Before Madeline could answer, Paige asked, "How about you? What have you enjoyed the most?"

"I think I liked the manicure best," Madeline answered. "My nails always look as if I've just been digging in the backyard, and my

Chapter Six: *Delightful*

hands stay so dry from washing dishes. I hope the conditioner we soaked in will take care of that for a day or two."

The two were quiet for a moment, basking in the ambiance of perfect peace and relaxation.

Finally Madeline spoke up. "When do you think we can do this again?" she asked.

"How about every other month?" suggested Paige.

"I could live with that," Madeline sighed. "But what about in the winter? Could we do this in the winter, too?"

Instead of answering, Paige suddenly bolted up from her chair. Through an open window she could hear the clock on the kitchen wall chiming three o'clock.

"Madeline, the time!" she cried, forgetting to catch the cucumbers as they fell from her eyes onto the patio floor. "Quick, go rinse your face. We only have half an hour before we have to pick up the kids from school. Then I have to pick up the baby from Mom's house."

Madeline jumped up, dropping her cucumbers on the floor next to her lounge chair. "Dump the water down the driveway so the bath salts won't kill the grass," she said, helping Paige drag the kiddie pool from the patio around the house to the driveway. They tipped one end, and the scent of freesia cascaded down the concrete into the street. With a sigh, Paige pulled the pool back into the shed behind the house while Madeline grabbed up the empty containers from the lunch they'd purchased from the grocery store that morning. She quickly tossed the plastic tubs and lids into the trash can next to the garage, stuffing them under a dirty diaper.

After a few quick minutes in the bathroom, the two friends had removed the last traces of Oil of Olay and were ready to climb into their cars for the trip that would signal a return to their everyday routine.

"Wait!" Paige cried before opening her car door. Madeline watched as her friend disappeared around the house and returned, holding up the four slices of cucumber that had fallen onto the patio. Paige dropped the slices into the trash can, and the two friends smiled at each other, satisfied that no traces of their self-indulgence remained.

With a quick hug, they climbed into their cars and drove off, one following the other to the elementary school just a few blocks away. Each friend wore a big smile, remembering the details of the delightful day they'd just shared—and dreaming of the next one.

PROVERBS 27:9

Perfume and incense bring joy

to the heart,

and the pleasantness of one's friend

springs from his earnest counsel.

Cheerfulness and contentment
are great beautifiers and
are famous preservers of youthful looks.

—Charles Dickens

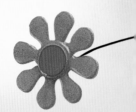

There is no cosmetic for beauty

like happiness.

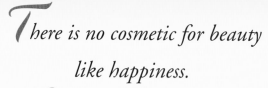

— Marguerite,
Countess of Blessington

He will yet fill your mouth

with laughter

and your lips

with shouts of joy.

—Job 8:21

Forever
Real
Inspiring
Encouraging
Never Failing
Delightful
Supportive

CHAPTER 7

Supportive

Storms are a fact of nature. The rains come, and the winds blow; and any tree in the path of that storm, if it does not have a strong root system to support it, is likely to be toppled.

Storms are a fact of life as well. Hard times come, and challenging circumstances threaten to topple us. But if we have the support of true friends, we not only survive; we thrive and grow.

Thanks for all your support. You are a true friend.

E Z R A   1 0 : 4

Rise up;

this matter is in your hands.

We will support you,

so take courage

and do it.

*Friendship is born at that moment
when one person says to another,
"What! You, too? I thought I was the only one."*

— C. S. Lewis

Do two walk together unless they have agreed to do so?

—Amos 3:3

NOT IN VAIN

If I can stop one heart from breaking,
I shall not live in vain:
If I can ease one life the aching,
Or cool one pain,
Or help one fainting robin
Unto his nest again,
I shall not live in vain.

—Emily Dickinson

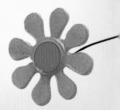

$\mathcal{A}$ friend is a person with whom

I may be sincere.

Before him, I may think aloud.

—*Ralph Waldo Emerson*